M000032448

STREAMS
IN DRY LAND

STREAMS IN DRY LAND

Praying when God is distant

Heather Ward

eagle

Guildford, Surrey

British Library Cataloguing-in-Publication Data. A catalogue
record for this book is available from the British Library.

Published by Eagle, an imprint of Inter Publishing Service (IPS)
Ltd, 59 Woodbridge Road, Guildford, Surrey GU1 4RF.

Typeset by The Electronic Book Factory Ltd, Fife, Scotland

Printed by Thomson Press (India) Limited

Cover design by Diana Overton

ISBN 0 86347 104 8

Contents

Foreword

I sometimes think of the books in this Exploring Prayer series as companions. And I often liken prayer to a voyage.

I remember the beginning of my own voyage well. It felt like embarking on a ship in the full blaze of the afternoon sun. I felt full of anticipation, awe and the awareness that God is as mysterious as the liquid gold sea across which I was travelling. I luxuriated in the glory, majesty, and felt love of God.

But then, just as day turns to pitch-black night and night engulfs a ship in darkness, prayer became dark and difficult. The heightened sense of God's love seemed to have dropped into the ocean like the setting sun. God seemed to have disappeared.

Had I done something to drive him away? How long would this darkness last? What should I do now? I was trapped. The ship continued to plough its way across the relentless sea. I could neither disembark nor find lasting pleasure in the voyage.

I was fortunate. I had a 'soul friend' to whom I could describe my disillusionment. I remember with gratitude the kindess and sensitivity with which he explained that the glory and the darkness, the fullness and emptiness are all normal. And I remember the twinkle in his eyes as he assured me that God had not disappeared; that I would see him peeping through or over or round the clouds again.

Would it be possible to find an author who could give readers a similar assurance? That was the question I asked myself as I planned this series of books on prayer. And that was when I thought of Heather Ward. We both lived in Nottingham at the time. People I respect spoke so highly of her that I read her first book, *The Gift of Self*. Then I heard her lecture on the subject of prayer and spirituality. I valued her insights and admired her honesty and discernment. I sensed that, if anyone could write on the subject of despair, she could.

Would she have the time? Would she even be interested in journeying with readers in this way?

To my delight, she accepted my invitation to contribute to the series and many readers will thank her for providing them with a book which they can consult when the pilgrimage of prayer leaves them bored, frustrated or in darkness. For, like the friend who came alongside me, Heather has shown that these feelings are quite normal – even appropriate to our journey into God. With humility and honesty, she reveals how she, too, has been becalmed by them from time to time. With the sensitivity which springs from such vulnerability, she suggests how we might view and cope with these phases of the journey, explains what is happening at such times and encourages us to remain on board even when excitement evaporates and the voyage seems endless and tedious.

Many readers, too, will reiterate my husband's verdict: 'It's the best book I've read for a long time.'

Joyce Huggett

Chapter 1

Praying when God has gone away

How long, O Lord? Wilt thou forget me forever?
How long wilt thou hide thy face from me?
(Psalm 13:1)

'When I was first converted I never seemed to stop praying but now it's hopeless. I can't pray and it's the last thing I want to do.'

'Prayer times used to be enjoyable, I felt so close to God but now it's just as though I am talking to myself.'

'In the past I used to feel so peaceful when I prayed; it made me feel good and almost, well, kind of holy but now there is just nothing. It's as though I had imagined it all.'

I wonder if these or similar thoughts have ever been yours or if you have ever felt that in some way or other your prayer has changed for the worse. There cannot be many of us who could honestly claim that our life with God has been without the odd hiccup. We know life doesn't work like that; we know *we* don't work like that.

It's not always easy to admit this, though. We often tend to put our relationship with God into a separate category from the rest of our lives. We can be inclined to think that, God being perfect, our life with him, to be authentic, must be hitch-free. If it's not, there is something wrong. We can forget too easily that we pray as human beings and as human beings we go up and down according to our moods, our daily experiences, our health. Because we are fallible our relationship with God is likely to follow, in part, the pattern of our relationship with people: left to ourselves we know nothing better. Because we are imperfect and created beings in relationship with our Creator who is all that we aren't – perfect and unchanging – that relationship is also likely, in part, to contradict our existing pattern. He leads us into his way of doing things. In the end our experience of prayer spans that apparent gulf, that contradiction between the God-who-is-with-us and the God-who-is-beyond-us. In Jesus God has become 'like us' and yet always remains 'other' to us, beyond our grasp. When our prayer collapses into emptiness, when from our human viewpoint we are left to our own devices, we often find we are being led across this gulf and being weaned from our dependence upon our pattern of human relationships and introduced into God's pattern.

Sometimes in this state it's of little immediate help to turn to some of the 'classics' of spiritual literature. The big, intense and dramatic experiences of which they speak can seem so remote from our daily struggle with a sense of futility, with our feelings of God's rejection or of our inability for any real knowledge of him. The great images of dark nights and deserts may strike chords and yet seem too vast, too romantic, for the grubby and petty reality of our lives. We feel dried-up, we feel there is no nourishment, no drop of refreshing water, but our world is small and harsh and urban, lacking the grandeur of the desert wastes. God no longer seems to be there, or if he is, we no longer have any conscious desire to reach out towards him. We find ourselves 'going through the motions' of a 'spiritual life'. The overwhelming dullness and monotony of our days, to which this gives rise, may seem too grey, too inconsequential, to qualify for grand terms like 'dark night of the senses'. And yet this is what it is, a time of grace when God is leading us out of reliance upon our human ways of understanding relationship and into his. It sounds contradictory but, to get this experience into perspective, it can often help to take a close look at the life-history of our closest human friendships. It's only by having a good idea of the normal life-cycle of our relationships that we can come to understand what we are bringing to our prayer and what God is doing in response.

When I look at my marriage for example, I can identify brief honeymoon periods of great, effortless closeness. These intersperse with times when we seem to jog along in an apparently routine affection and fidelity. We are unaware of much happening between us in terms of emotional 'highs' but neither is there any dissatisfaction. Love is a matter of mutual concern, contentment and security which has little impact on our emotions. There is no thrill of being 'in love' but our daily living speaks of an unvoiced closeness.

Then the needs or mood of one of us change. Pressure at work, anxiety about the future or pain from the past may take one of us over. The resulting withdrawal into a shell leaves the other to do all the running in the relationship, usually by more or less patient waiting for the phase to pass.

Sometimes the apparent routine, rather than being rudely interrupted, slowly declines into an absorption with these problems. The daily habits persist but their meaning is forgotten in the need to keep oneself going. Sometimes the awareness of love, rather than gushing out in grand gesture, seeps through into little things, into the gestures, the actions, the kindnesses which set the tone of daily life.

Some of these changes seem to come with seasonal regularity. Perhaps we recognise that around the anniversary of a death one of us is more withdrawn or that for one of us the onset of winter darkness and winter smells arouses nameless fears and forebodings.

Others stem from particular circumstances. Our daughter's temporary unhappiness at school awakens memories we'd sooner squash. A prolonged spell of being under the weather leaves one of us mildly depressed, with energy sufficient only for day-to-day existence.

At other times one of us is 'on top of the world' because something has gone well at work, nagging worries have been dispelled or simply because the sun is shining: as a result our relationship feels equally vibrant.

I'm sure we could all trace our own pattern of ups and downs in friendships. I'd be surprised if we couldn't, for all these responses boil down to one fact – we are human; our body, emotions, memories, personality inevitably direct our relationships. This is the common human stuff which we bring to any friendship, with people or with God. Just because in prayer we are meeting One who is beyond our limitations does not mean that these no longer exist. We go to the meeting with him as we are so that he can gradually make us as he is. As we grow in friendship with him inevitably we find that we go through all the ups and downs experienced in our love for another person. Yet there is one difference – his response. God does not blow hot and cold with us. He does not withdraw into himself in pain or pique or panic nor does he jog along keeping us happy with twenty percent of himself. God lavishes all of himself upon us all of the time.

As I've been writing these last sentences I've protested: 'That's not what I feel – he does withdraw! He picks me up and puts me down as he feels like it!' My mind agrees with all I say while my feelings rebel. And that's our problem, isn't it? We are stuck, so often, in our human habit of interpreting everything through our feelings. My human limitation and changeability don't affect only what I bring to my relationship with God they also affect my interpretation of what God puts into it. My feelings tell me that God is doing to me what I do to him and to others, while my mind says that he acts otherwise.

Mind and feelings do agree, however, that there are phases in this growing friendship with God which cannot be put down to my moods. If they can't be attributed to his moods either what is their cause? The answer lies, of course, in the fact that this relationship is not between equals. I am a creature, dependent, contingent, and he is one whose 'thoughts are not our thoughts and ways not our ways' (see Isaiah 55:8–10).

Growing in prayer is like learning a new language, God's language; it has a grammar, a vocabulary, an idiom unlike any we have ever encountered. Our relationship with him begins in our language of feelings and dependence upon moods and gradually moves into his language, a language of the spirit beyond change, beyond mood, beyond emotion. It's inevitable, therefore, that communication will often seem impossible. We don't know enough of his language but for our own progress in it, he will no longer use ours.

As with the process of becoming like a native-speaker of any language it's not just a matter of learning new vocabulary and grammar but also of getting to know the world of the person who uses it. We have to be ready to abandon our usual way of seeing, expressing and experiencing what is happening within and around us. Take, for example, an English person learning to speak the Inuit (Eskimo) language and encountering their hundred or so different words for snow. He has to learn not only the words but a new way of seeing, so that he recognises the differing states to which they refer. More than that he has also to appreciate from the inside the conditions and way of life which make these distinctions so important. His acquisition of his new language involves his letting go of his customary attitude 'snow's snow' and of all the expectations of his environment accompanying it.

At times this kind of learning is exhilarating, when we break through to a new understanding, to a new capacity to achieve communication. At others it's painful and frustrating: we feel we will never catch on, that we cannot adjust to this new way of seeing things, that things are happening to which we cannot respond. We are stuck in and with ourselves, in and with our ways.

It is the same with praying. Our dry, empty and bleak phases often come when we are stuck in ourselves, when we cling to our own ways by looking for pleasure and reassurance in prayer. They occur when we want to give and receive only in our language of feeling and emotion. They occur when we have lost our desire to communicate in our language but do not yet know enough of God's to speak in his. We are left tongue-tied, useless, unable to return to using the one while incapable of speaking the other.

Often God treats us as any sympathetic host might help a guest living with him to learn his language. Initially there's great indulgence, a lot of the guest's native language is spoken until familiarity increases. Then the frequency diminishes and the guest is more and more obliged to use his new language unless fatigue, frustration or circumstance invites a return to the familiar. There will be critical moments when the host knows he must leave his guest to suffer and flounder or he will never consolidate the level of fluency he is approaching. The host watches over him anxiously, protects him from his worst errors and provides the experiences he needs but does not intervene directly. His patience is rewarded when at last his guest begins to speak spontaneously, unaware of what he is doing, at home in his new tongue.

This final stage is the combination of several smaller, similar leaps from one way of knowing the language to another. Each involves loss of some kind, for spontaneity implies a lack of awareness of our actions. As we grow in knowledge so often we no longer 'know that we know': this applies to any language, to any skill, it applies also to our coming to friendship with God on *his* terms, speaking *his* language.

In learning a foreign tongue, the deeper our knowledge of grammar, idiom, dialect, through our use of it, the less we are involved in translation, in consciously selecting the right word. We may not even think that we know the proper expression until we find ourselves saying it. The language has become part of us. It is no longer a package of knowledge and skills which we self-consciously possess and use. In a sense we may feel the poorer for it, for we no longer have the sense of being stocked up with knowledge, of being in control of this capacity for communication. Instead of our making conscious use of the language it is as though it uses us.

In our friendship with God it is much the same. Usually we know of him initially through ideas which satisfied our minds or emotions. Gradually we come to know him as, perhaps, Healer, Saviour, Friend. We experience something of his identity; we feel we know whom we are meeting in prayer. But as the relationship grows, the 'knowledge' of him becomes increasingly part of us and we can no longer recognise him in the labels and ideas previously attached to him. We can no longer feel spiritually rich and stocked up as we did, perhaps, when our imagination produced vivid meditations and allowed us to respond emotionally to a recreated Gospel scene. We are left with a simple, bare appreciation of truth and love which we know, even if we cannot feel it, has its source in Jesus. This feels like a decline, like a loss, when we have simply moved, like the linguist, from consciously possessing knowledge, our ideas and images of God, into living in a knowledge which is part of us.

Our times of darkness, our periods when prayer is flat or stale and God seems absent without leave, are part and parcel of our human living and of our movement into the life of God. We can be too ready to make much of these phases if we do not understand them properly. We all know, I suspect, the temptation to make our grey patches the excuse for 'getting off God's hook', and living an 'ordinary' life like everyone else, without this constant longing for something more. We so readily tell ourselves that this bleakness is proof that our earlier experience was illusory and it's sheer self-delusion to carry on, knowing the uselessness of it all.

For those of us who know something of the mystical tradition comes the opposite temptation; darkness and aridity are sure signs of God's special dealing with us. Any emptiness or bleakness, therefore, is a proof of special election, of being a favoured soul. We twist the experience to flatter and enlarge our ego.

We can so easily use these experiences to gratify either our sloth, our reluctance to answer God's call, or our pride, our conviction of our own greatness. Our one reason for exploring our 'dry land' is to enable us to resist these temptations and to confirm us in the truth that we are all wounded, sinful people whom God desires to transform into saints. Darkness and aridity in our prayer keep us in humble awareness of the truth of our wretchedness and in joyful hope of salvation.

**But I am like a deaf man,
I do not hear (Psalm 38:13)**

The old saying has it, 'There's none so deaf as those who will not hear.' Tell your busy child it's time for bed or your partner it's their turn to wash the dishes or clean the car and you are left in no doubt of its truth. We hear selectively: sometimes we hear what we choose to hear, sometimes what we expect to hear, at other times what we are free to hear. Our capacity to receive any communication often depends on these three factors – our will, our expectations, our freedom from 'interference' from preoccupations, memories and fears. How often have we got the wrong end of the stick because our conversation hasn't gone as we'd anticipated and so we have gone away with what we wanted to hear only to find that the opposite is actually happening? How often we meet elderly people who complain that they have seen no-one, despite the daily visits of nurses and home helps, because none of the longed-for relatives have called. How often we find that friends with low self-esteem never register anything positive which is said about them. Their low opinion of themselves stops their hearing: there is too much 'noise' from the painful impressions received in childhood preventing it.

These factors affect our everyday hearing and receiving, they are at work in our human relationships; they also affect our communication with God in prayer.

Often staleness and dryness come upon us in prayer without any warning. The sense of God's closeness, the awareness of his love or his holiness suddenly disappear and we are left feeling nothing except the vague absurdity of our situation. We try to 'gee' ourselves up with Scripture reading but that falls flat: passages that would at other times have had us dancing on the ceiling or weeping buckets now leave us cold and unmoved. Praying is a chore, reading leaves us bored, our lives in general seem to offer nothing but a vista of endless sameness. Deep down we feel vaguely resentful of God, we expected better of him. We feel he should make us feel we're doing something useful in praying, something which will bring some zip and colour into our lives. The dryness begins to expose our 'hidden agenda' with God: in return for our worship and attention we really expect him to make our lives 'happy' and satisfying. Our desire for God is at least partially a desire for what he can do for us – do for us in ways which we can immediately and effortlessly apprehend.

So, when our prayer grows bleak and empty, often God is pushing us to examine our expectations of him and to come to a new understanding of the meaning of love. As we have seen, he shows us the self-love involved in our love for him, but he also leads us to a new approach to our capacity for choice.

When aridity strikes we can give up praying, turn to 'good works' which make us feel better or we can plod on faithfully without seeing much sense in what we are doing. As in a human partnership we can continue in a day-to-day fidelity without any of the feelings we would call 'love'. Yet such it is. Our human ideas of love are inextricably linked with emotions, with sensations, with much that is irrational; they feed back into our earliest experiences when we were, literally, all feeling.

In prayer, as in any authentic relationship, God teaches us his meaning of love which is a matter of choice, of will. It does involve a passion, a suffering, a longing for us which comes out of his choice of us, out of the exercise of his free will in creating and redeeming us. It's a passion far removed from the self-gratification and irrationality that word suggests when applied to our experience.

Frequently our staleness in prayer arises from a clash between these two understandings of love. We expect to receive a love we can register with our feelings and return likewise. He continues to love us by choosing what is better for us – an opportunity to learn to love by choosing relationship in indifference to emotional rewards. We can make ourselves blind and deaf to God's presence then, by waiting for and expecting what will please us. The cause of our dryness lies in us: the Lord uses it to bring us gradually out of our kind of loving and into his.

How much expectation may make us deaf to what the Lord is doing with us I learnt graphically some years ago. For a long while I had had a great desire for solitude and 'exposure' to God, without being entirely sure what such exposure would entail. I'm sure I was thinking of something rather grand, if painful. Eventually I was able to spend a few days in the hermitage of a city-centre convent, where solitude could be combined with participation in the daily office, including the midnight vigil. It was to be wonderful, all I wanted. But nothing is as one expects.

Physical inactivity made me soon cold. The absence of the regular demands on my time made me quickly feel aimless. I became obsessed by thoughts of mealtimes to break up the day and of means of defeating the cold. Worse still was my long-repressed fear of the dark – I began to imagine intruders climbing over the convent walls and hiding in the slightly tumbledown shed linking hermitage to convent courtyard. Go to midnight office? Not me, I hid quaking beneath my blankets. My grand desire for solitude with God had collapsed into surrender to basic animal needs and infantile irrationality. I had fooled myself into expecting great heights only to be left to dabble in the shallow puddle of my pettiness, my attachment to creature comforts and my fearfulness. Initially I was tempted to abandon the attempt as a flop but I stayed and came to realize that this was, indeed, exposure to God. I had arrived looking, unconsciously, for gratification, for fulfilment of a fantasy: he had offered, instead, to show me myself in his light, to expose where I had been using him as an escape from the poverty of my inner self. I went home with my self-made wings clipped, yet happy. In this dry land I had met the God of Truth.

Sometimes, like the busy child at bedtime, we are subconsciously deaf to God because somewhere we are choosing not to listen. This can often happen at a growth point in our relationship with him: perhaps we fear the cost of deeper commitment, perhaps we shrink from the necessary surrender of a long-cherished habit or ambition. Turning off is one way of avoiding the issue: we do not wish to hear God on this subject but, since everything seems to speak of it, the only solution is withdrawal into oneself.

Again, this experience tests our will. What do we really want? We need to open ourselves to the possibility that our desert results from wanting not to hear God. We have to be as honest as we can with him. We want to love him yet we don't want to know what we are refusing to hear. We want him on our terms. We have to be content simply to rest before him in this predicament, to let the dry land we inhabit expose our truth to his light. We have to be content to be without a hiding-place so that he can probe us and discover the place in us where we can say 'yes' to him. This waiting, this refusal to be anywhere else, this readiness to be known by him in our uselessness and rebellion is our love for God, choosing what is required for relationship with him, when our feelings tell us the enterprise is useless.

Sometimes our choice is of deafness not to God but to ourselves. Feelings and responses are developing within us which we would sooner ignore. Unwittingly we censor ourselves drastically by closing down altogether: opening ourselves to God would mean experiencing all those things we deem 'bad' and unacceptable. We would dearly like to listen to God provided we did not need to listen to the mess, the pain, the fury within; provided we could continue feeling 'better' people through our prayer. Often, depending upon our tradition and temperament, we may tend to think that our 'conversion' should have entirely destroyed the 'old man'. We may look to prayer to confirm these expectations and it is a nasty shock when they are not met. Here we are, sincerely endeavouring to give ourselves to God, and look where it has landed us, in the grip of all the stirrings of the old Adam.

Given this belief about what we, and the venture of prayer, *should* be, it is hardly surprising that we end up simply sitting on ourselves. We daren't respond to God lest the cracks show in the Christian façade we are sure he wants. Worse still, the repression of our feelings, plus our sense of failure, can lead to a mild depression in which everything feels dull, lifeless and flat. What begins as a 'problem with prayer' shows itself to have deeper roots in our inability to accept our human nature and to believe that God also accepts it in order to transform it.

So, frequently we make a fertile place into a desert for ourselves because we do not understand that 'before God brings peace he first makes war'. Growing in friendship with him brings up in us all that rebels against, all that passively resists, all that is indifferent and careless towards, him. This is what needs healing in us and it cannot be done while we try to behave as though we were well. I suspect that one kind of darkness in prayer is akin to the experience of the patient who is disappointed after a medical consultation. Behind the complaint of its uselessness lies the reality that all attempts to elicit information about symptoms were met by bland denials of any problem. Anxiety about his health has led him to conceal, rather than reveal, his condition. Like the patient who fears the worst we must be prepared to let Jesus the healer know all our nasty symptoms and probe our deepest wounds.

This is not easy. Often we can let it happen only in stages, gradually trusting him with a little more of our unacceptable selves. At times the pain, the feelings, the memories we are sitting upon may be too big for us to handle alone and we need to ask for outside help. If this happens we can again be tempted to feel failures – prayer has not built us up but broken us down, so surely something is wrong with this whole endeavour? We need to hold firmly to the certainty that God is not withdrawing from us owing to our awfulness, but intervening powerfully in our lives to make our hidden wounds accessible to healing.

We can see how our expectations and our choices have led to lack of freedom to hear and receive the Lord. We have supplied ourselves with spiritual and psychological blinkers and earplugs, as it were. Often, however, we lose our freedom of response because we have become too absorbed by memories of past relationships; these may further shape our choices and expectations or simply leave no space within us for God.

Memory and expectation are closely linked, aren't they? What we expect in the present and the future frequently derives from what we have received and experienced in the past, especially in our formative childhood years.

It is often said that our earliest notions of heaven and hell come out of our early knowledge of the world. When we begin the search for God these early memories can easily be aroused. Confusion between relationship with God and relationship with parents readily occurs. We can tend to look, unconsciously, for the warmth and closeness we had with a parent when we come to God in prayer. Part of the pleasure in the early stages of praying may well have emerged out of mixing our awareness of God's love for us with our earliest memories of being totally loved as a baby. I think God allows these initially because they stir up the desire for him in us and attract us further to him; after all, the love of our parents *is* a reflection of his love for us. It is as though we are responding to his love mediated to us through memories of these important people because we still need tangible evidence of it; our senses are still involved in our understanding of love. As we grow closer to him the power of these memories fades. We are maturing into a degree of independence from our feelings but the loss of them troubles us, it seems like a regression, as though we no longer love.

Wilt thou forget me forever?

For many people, however, it is memory of the loss, or absence of the parent which is triggered in our relationship with God. These memories are often experienced more strongly when it is God who seems to be abandoning the relationship but they may also be a factor in our 'turning off' from him.

We can frequently begin by seeking in prayer, compensation for the deprivations and denials of our childhood. At last we have someone who loves unconditionally, whose love and power to sustain never fail! Memories of love given then withdrawn, of food and comfort scanty or unpredictable in supply, begin to stir. Without realising it we can slip back into our earliest state and let God truly re-mother us. This is good and necessary; we have to allow him to fill the (literally) crying needs in us as he sees fit. Once more, however, as the 'parent-gaps' begin to diminish, the strong experience of being loved in prayer can fade. Our desire for God for himself begins to dominate the inevitable desire for him for what he does for us. Spiritually there is growth but emotionally we feel the loss of that singular intensity in our longing for God. Frequently the child within us reacts with characteristic self-blame, 'It's my fault God has gone away, it's something I've done!' The resulting panic and dejection may further lock us into ourselves and thus deepen our aridity, for we are able to see only our perceived failure and not the goodness of the Lord who is no longer feeding us with the milk of the healing of our memories but with the strong meat of his reality.

Memories, too, can revive not only desire but also revulsions. Childhood memories of neglectful or intrusive care may have led to an often deeply hidden mistrust of loving and being loved. As the Paul Simon song says 'If I'd never loved I never would have cried.' The business of loving may be so closely linked with the recollection of pain, physical or emotional, that we find our desert results from the 'No Entry' sign marking our inmost being. We want God but, in the depths of our personality, lies this fear that to let him in would mean our annihilation. We end up in a catch-22 situation – to avoid becoming the wasteland of our earliest memories, through surrender to a devouring, destructive 'god', we make of ourselves a present desert, closing our ears to the

voice of One who comes to restore and not to lay waste. All we can do in this situation is to learn, slowly and painfully, to recognize the memories (which by now are close to fantasies), to identify the false god they have created and to put all our energy into affirming our belief in the loving, sustaining and healing power of the true God, whatever we feel. We have to unmask the memory for what it now is, a lie, while recognizing the truth of its original causation, so that we can consciously, with our will, invite the Lord beyond our barricades.

Acknowledging that in prayer we may be experiencing not God but ourselves, in terms of our memories and hang-ups, can seem very threatening. To meet the suggestion that our search for God is mixed with so much psychological baggage from the past, just when we are already feeling the 'loss' of God, can be devastating. We can begin to wonder whether there is any reality in anything we experience. Yet again, false expectations lie at the heart of our problem. We can too readily fall into the expectation that we are angels in prayer, that our bodies, our temperaments and all our life in the world are set aside when we come to the Lord. We are like the labourers in the parable, who are perplexed to find both wheat and tares in our fields. We have expected to find nothing but the wheat of our spiritual nature and now the sight of the tares of our human woundedness threatens to blind us to the existence of the wheat.

Initially in prayer God often draws us to himself by allowing us to see the wheat. Gradually he begins to deal with the tares, slowly breaking their connection with their roots. The loosening of the earth around them shakes our foundations. We feel as though we are 'going to pieces,' the tares grab our attention and it seems as though it is the wheat which has been dislodged. When we look at the poor field of our self it seems to be nothing but weeds.

This began to dawn on me some years ago, shortly after a second 'conversion'[1]. Quite high from the experience, I was intoxicated with the vision of Man's destiny and aboard the 'glory train'. I say 'high' deliberately because I did feel like a kite, made to soar into the heights, made for heaven, not for earth. Vaguely I knew that the kite was anchored, was not free, but at that point was little troubled by it. Then suddenly my kite string was cut and flew away but it didn't take me with it. I was left in the 'lump', the dead weight which I now realized had been holding down the kite. I was totally earth-bound, immersed in this inert mass. It didn't pull away from God but simply resisted by being its

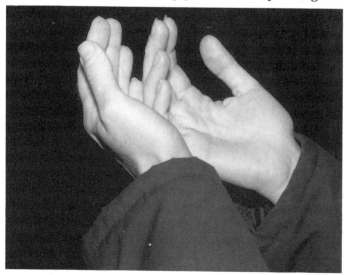

own heavy, unyielding self. At last I began to realize that I had been separating what belonged together, our spiritual nature, ourselves as made-for-God, made-for-glory, and ourselves as fallen people whose physical and psychological make-up can so often render us resistant and inert towards God. Whenever I had sunk into depression I had become all 'lump', unable to maintain sight of the kite. Whenever I emerged from it I would strive to forget the lump in concentration on the kite. I was experiencing the two in 'either-or' terms because this was how I expected it to be. I had to learn to appreciate that the kite existed, in fact, *within* the lump and that its purpose was not to fly off as pure spirit to Spirit but to lighten the heaviness of the lump with its aspiration towards God and to ensure its Godward movement, so that ultimately the whole would be heaven-bound.

I came to understand this only by accepting what I felt was unacceptable, that is, that the lump was the truth of our human condition and it was that condition and no other which the Lord had redeemed. Present perfection was just not part of the deal. It became increasingly clear that the Lord who came in the silence as free gift was not waiting for this muddled, divided, immature and sinful woman to cease being all these things before he invited her to friendship nor did he expect that they would quickly be left behind in her faltering efforts to respond. Praying was simply to hold ourselves open to him, to invite him into the chaos and the nothingness which threaten to overwhelm us whenever we glimpse them. It was to give him freedom to do with the mess anything he saw fit, accepting that his work in us could not be a journey into his light without also

being a journey into our own darkness. Increasingly I learnt the truth, at the spiritual level, of Thomas Carlyle's remark, 'All chaos is order shaping itself free.' Giving our consent to God's creating and re-creating power in our darkness, in our formless void, becomes then the main focus for our prayer.

Expectations of angelic status can also lead us to ignore the contribution of our physical health to our experience of darkness and lack of interest in the things of God. Physical illness and its after-effects are notoriously depressing; pain, and the struggle against it, can so often take us over so completely that there is no apparent room for awareness of anything else. When we feel we are simply drag-ging ourselves around, the struggle to keep going can readily squeeze out apparent awareness of our desire for God. Notice I say 'apparent room' and 'apparent awareness' of our desire. Our feelings of staleness can frequently arise from, or be deepened by, our impatient insistence on knowing or feeling the effects of our relationship with God. We think our prayer should be above being influenced by our bodies and so disregard it as a possible source for the feeling of having left our spiritual phone off the hook. We expect to know what is going on between God and ourselves, so that the absence of tangible contact implies the absence of relationship. It is hard for us to appreciate that our communication with God may merely have gone underground, as it were, sustaining the roots of the relationship, while the surface is preoccupied by immediate needs.

What is asked of us in this situation is not to force ourselves into conscious prayer but to rest in the certainty that he is bigger than we are, that he can carry us in this relationship until we are able to be more responsive. Such resting *is* a prayer of faith and abandonment for it asks us to surrender ourselves to the existence of a relationship for which we have no immediate evidence. It asks us to exercise the continual contradiction of faith to feeling by our affirmation that we are in God's hands when our emotional state tells us we have removed ourselves from them.

Throughout every aspect of these times when we have ostensibly turned-off from God he is calling us to deeper faith, deeper truthfulness, deeper humility. Constantly he is challenging us to set his promises, his mercy, his everlasting love above our own feelings, expectations, illusions, memories. He asks us to set more store by his fidelity to us, his everlasting covenant with us, than by our infidelities. He calls us to live in the truth of humility, that is, in the truth of our messy and muddled humanity which is groaning for liberation from bondage (cf. Romans 8:21). He wants us to love and embrace the truth of our littleness and inability to 'bear much reality', so that we look only to him for salvation. That is, he wants us, most of all, through this experience of darkness to surrender our desire to be O.K. people and to live in acceptance of his power to make silk purses from the sows' ears of our lives. This is his speciality: experience of aridity, of deafness, of lack of freedom to respond to him, is the invitation to supply him with the necessary material.

Why do you hide your face?

So far we have been looking at a darkness and dryness in prayer which seems to stem from difficulties from our side in this friendship with God. There remain, however, experiences of spiritual desert, of blankness, of bleakness which seem visited on us. We are all attentiveness, all longing, but God has gone absent without leave, has shut up shop and left no forwarding address. The desire for him is strong in us, the awareness of our need overwhelming and yet we can find no evidence of his interest in us or even no evidence of his existence. At times he seems absent only from our lives and we fret at the signs of his actions in others. At others it's as though he has abandoned the world altogether, withdrawn his life-giving Spirit, so that everything seems dry and dead, ready to fall into nothingness. At yet other times, it is as though God has exiled us: we know *that* he is but he is not with us, he has sent us away and we respond with new recognition to the cry of the psalmist:

By the waters of Babylon, there we sat down and wept, when we remembered Zion.
How shall we sing the Lord's song in a foreign land?

(Psalm 137:1, 4)

We seem to have been cast-off in a foreign and godless land.

If the experience of our own deafness to God brings pain it is usually the suffering involved with lethargy, with boredom. We feel dulled and incapable of registering much response, an experience which often grows into the pain of confusion and doubt. Ultimately, of course, it leads us to the pain involved in repentance, in knowing what we are without God. When it is God himself who is absent the suffering is often more acute and more intense. We are grieving a loss; something has been cut off from us and we are left incomplete and vulnerable.

I once remarked to a young student how much it hurt to know that God existed and had yet forgotten us. He was astounded. For him this would have been welcome freedom: God had a claim on us, how lucky to be overlooked and so excused payment! Sometimes when the pain of God's absence is great the student seems to have a point. To stop wanting God because he has (apparently) ceased wanting us would be a release. Yet, deep down, we know that to stop wanting him would be worse than to die: like St. Peter we know we have nowhere else to go:

Jesus said to the twelve, 'Will you also go away?'
Simon Peter answered him, 'Lord, to whom shall
we go? You have the words of eternal life; and
we have believed, and have come to know, that
you are the Holy One of God.'

(John 6:67–69)

The truth is that we cannot stop wanting God; when the prospect of 'release' seems a reality the resulting void appals us. He has touched us, claimed us, caught us in the net of his love and mercy. To live outside it would be unthinkable. Yet living in it when awareness of that love and mercy are withdrawn reduces it to a simple snare, bringing scarcely bearable pain. We are caught between a rock and a hard place.

So we have to keep longing for God even though it seems hopeless. We feel discarded, as though found out in our uselessness and left in a corner, or as though we were an outgrown toy.

At other times we are reminded of those days in adolescence when we had prepared for hours for a date with someone we had idolized for months only to be 'stood up', or when, after a holiday romance, we agonized every time the postman called without the longed-for letter. Time dragged and, though we may have forgotten our waiting temporarily, it remained nagging at the back of our minds, to return in full force whenever our minds were free.

It's not just the pain of unfulfilled longing which disturbs us, it's the reasons we find for our state, too. As teenagers we readily blamed ourselves – our acne, our looks, our clothes, our personality. As adults seeking God it's much the same. 'God is punishing me,' 'I'm not good enough.' We play Job's comforters with ourselves, trying to find an explanation for this in terms of reward and chastisement.

We dredge up each and every past sin and infidelity as though we were counting black marks in a punishment book and assessing the subsequent penalty. We remember all those people we've known who seem to have enjoyed themselves without God only to come to a bad end, reminding ourselves that every pleasure has its price. We try to 'balance the books' of our lives, as it were, so that what is happening to us seems entirely explicable and predictable according to our limited idea of justice.

Yet frequently, there is at the same time an inarticulate feeling that, like Job's, these explanations miss the point. We know our sinfulness and yet this experience seems bigger than such cause and effect arguments would allow. It doesn't seem to be a question simply of our own rupture from God: it seems all out of proportion, making us too big in the scheme of things. We seem to be getting more than our fair share, as though we were being singled out to take what belonged to everyone.

A sense of unfairness and disproportion: an apprehension of a crushing punishment for our sins. Do we really believe in a God who is unjust and merciless? Do we really have a God who simply discards his pots if they don't come up to scratch? Our minds may give a round 'no' in reply but our instinctive response might well be 'yes' or 'sometimes I think so.' Besides a Christian God in our hearts all too many of us also have a primitive, vengeful deity, who seems to come from our earliest attempts to make sense of our world and our earliest memories of being dependent creatures within it.

I think that this experience of being exiled from, or abandoned by God is often his way of revealing and expunging from our hearts this alternative god who distorts our understanding of, and response to, the God revealed in Jesus. Basic human religiousness apprehends a power beyond ourselves upon which we are dependent. Usually this is a power to be appeased and kept happy, a god of whim and moods, a punitive god who demands sacrifice. All these primitive intuitions are hooked-up in our experience of darkness: they come into the open and challenge our faith. The darkness, the dryness, the feeling of exile, are invitations to affirm our faith in a loving and merciful Father, a self-emptying elder brother, an abiding, life-giving Spirit, when this false, primitive god within us would have us believe in injustice and human sacrifice.

It brings to the surface, too, those memories of our early days which provide the pegs for some of our ideas about God. Very often our feelings of God's absence, of being abandoned, or shut out, have mixed in with them recollections of those times as a young, dependent being when the longed-for parent did not appear. That time of mother's illness or of a stay in hospital when visitors were forbidden might emerge or the stress resulting from rigid, yet well-intentioned, adherence to a regime of 'no-picking-up-or-you'll-spoil-the-baby'.

I am by no means suggesting that our experience of God's absence is, in fact, simply a memory of some kind of childhood deprivation; far from it. I do suggest, however, that echoes of painful early events resound in our times of darkness, lending them a particular anguish and leading us to false conclusions about the nature of God's dealings with us which affirm our inner false god.

I used to believe that it was absolutely vital not to confuse these two, that *real* experience of God's absence must be entirely distinguished in our hearts, minds and understanding from these early memories. Now I am not so sure. It seems to me that we can waste a lot of time and energy trying to discern which is which and become over-concerned about the 'authenticity' of what is happening to us. Certainly I have found it so. I have come to the conclusion that all that matters is that we acknowledge that all our experience is mixed, is 'contaminated' by our memories and our responses to them, and that we then, in some bit of us, however fragile and tiny, hold to the truth that God *is* Love, that anything which contradicts this faith is not of him. If we can do this, then, whatever the origin of our time of darkness or the cause of its innards-wrenching intensity, he can do something with it. We have to surrender our entire state to him, looking not at our feelings but

at what we believe about him, however puny and intangible that belief may seem. This desert asks us to give God the chance to *be* God, to be greater than our feelings, to be their great contradictor. If we can let him be in this way he can begin to free us from our illusions and fantasies which keep us from him.

I recall in such a period of bleakness being possessed by a repellent image. God was a spider who set out to attract and lure his prey into his web with his apparent love and beauty only to turn, once they were trapped, to reveal the full ugliness of his malicious evil. This persisted for a whole summer. At an earlier time, realising its primitive origin, I might have sought counselling help to 'work through' what this was about. Instead I simply allowed it to be in my mind without any conscious dwelling upon it. Though I could feel nothing of God's loving goodness I could only cling to the prayer 'Lord, I believe in your goodness, help my unbelief' (Mark 9:24). The image left me as suddenly as it had come but I had learnt through it just one of those fantasies which made me distrustful of God and fearful of being loved. The primitive message 'Love and be loved and you will be destroyed' was being reawakened in the experience of being loved and apparently abandoned by God. Staying with the image without attempting to analyse it had made me hear the message clearly for the first time but it had also begun to weaken its grip on me. Faith was beginning to get another toe-hold, there had been one more lesson in the contradiction between God's truth and the 'truth' of experience.

There are two important points here, I think, about this confusion between our memories and

God's actions in our lives. It is vital to accept that, from our point of view, it is well-nigh impossible to separate neatly the spiritual and the psychological. They *are* distinct but we know them only as a mixture; our temperaments, past, culture, education and upbringing all colour our interpretation of spiritual experience. We shouldn't then, disown pain in our 'spiritual life' as something psychological to be removed as quickly as possible or to be treated as having no bearing on our spirit. Everything which happens to us is grist for God's mill. We may need to seek a resolution of our problem but we need to do so with an eye and an ear to what God may be teaching us or doing with us in the process.

Conversely I think we must beware of claiming any experience as wholly spiritual: that is not for us to judge. We run the risk not only of elevating ourselves to illusory spiritual heights but we may miss, also, the psychological blocks in our way which God may wish to show us. Only humble acceptance of wheat and tares, kite and lump, offers God full scope in us, an acceptance which keeps us turned outward in waiting upon him and not inward in paralysed self-contemplation.

Having said that I would no longer delve too much into the origin of the false god revealed in our darkness, I need also to add that there may be times for some people when the psychological wound is so dominant that help is vital. I am thinking of those times when God's absence so much evokes memories of earlier rejection that the desire to live is seriously threatened or the rage at injustice seems uncontainable or the greyness becomes so all-pervasive as to destroy the capacity for hope. In these states our emotional wounds – or our physiological/chemical imbalance – are crying out for an attention they must not be denied.

Having suffered from clinical depression I know how easy it is at these times to dismiss the spiritual from the picture and to add the sense of being spiritually deficient to our feelings of psychological dereliction. It's tempting to assume that nothing in

this is really about God and that we must wait to be 'together' before any spiritual life is possible. I see now that such a view has no foundation. God is there, waiting for us at every moment in our lives and it is the places where we are most broken which may offer him greatest access. He lets no experience go to waste, if only we will give him freedom to act. If our longing for God opens up our wounds it is so that they may be cleansed and made open to him as Healer and Saviour.

So 'loss of God' exposes our inner false gods, brings to light some of the obstacles to our response to him. It purges our faith of reward and punishment religion, shows up the self-seeking within our search for God. Through this experience of his absence or of our exile, God leads us to a deeper faith and hope grounded not in what we can see, feel or know at any one moment but in pure adherence to his self-revelation in Scripture, in the church, in the world, which is bigger than ourselves. He asks of us a fidelity to that initial gift of faith which enables us to accept that revelation as truth. It means dethroning our feelings and our way of interpreting reality from its central place in our existence. If life is a gamble, it's a matter of putting all our stake on God.

It's a call to deeper faith and hope but it's also an invitation to a purer kind of love of God which defies concern for ourselves, here or in eternity. When God has gone away, leaving us in a dry and dusty land or when he seems to have packed us off to a foreign land, we have a choice. Do we 'curse God and die' or go on loving in the void? Do we answer rejection for rejection, indifference for indifference or do we say with the poet George Herbert:

Ah my dear God! though I am clean forgot,
Let me not love thee, if I love thee not.[2]

Is the worst we can imagine the pain we feel in being rejected or the pain of not loving him? The self-interest in our love for God is tried to the limits. We are brought face to face with our 'pagan' love which is only for our friends and benefactors (Matthew 5:46–47).

The darkness may well make us feel incapable of loving. God himself has been the source of our love so that without him nothing seems left to us. Nothing *is* left, of course, except our will. In the end we are led to the place where we must say 'I desire to love you even in hell.'

My heart within me is appalled
(Psalm 143:4)

All that I've said so far is about the times when we feel that the living God has abandoned us. He is, exists, but has left our personal world. Sometimes, however, it can seem more that God has 'died' or that he has never been more than a figment of our imaginations, a product of wishful thinking. Doubts come flooding in, the unanswered questions at the back of our minds leap to the forefront, clamouring for attention. Everything that happens in the wider world seems to be an assault on the shreds of our belief, hope and capacity for loving.

Sometimes this happens out of the blue but perhaps more often as the result of external events. Suffering or death of loved ones, the cracking of a marriage, the rebellion of a child, accumulated misfortunes such as debt, redundancy and ill health, may all call into question for us the reality of a loving God. In this mood whenever we look at the world we see only the violence, the cruelty, the inhuman rapacity and stupidity within it. The question surges up: 'Is this truly humankind in the image of God?' When human beings behave like monsters and God seems indifferent to them, the less painful solution in our darkness may well seem to be simple acceptance of apparent meaninglessness and the adoption of a seemingly more rational, if hope-less, attitude to existence.

I know this particular temptation all too well. I have come to realize that if, with one shred of my being, I can maintain the possibility that God is bigger than my mind and my despair, he can use this darkness to purge further distorted images of him.

Deep down within us there seems to be a desire for God the watchmaker, who has absolute control over all his working parts. Or we want God the magician, correcting everything with a wave of his wand. We want the Garden of Eden but without any of the apparent restrictions. God must be God in ensuring absolute peace and plenty while we are utterly free to act as independent beings with no responsibility to Creator or creation. We don't like the mess which goes with our freedom. We don't want suffering, we don't want violence, we don't want conflict and so we demand a God who will deal with all of this from the outside, instantaneously and without our involvement. We want a God who will make things

better in the way our mothers dealt with our knocks as children, with a 'magic' rub and a kiss. Only now we are like the child who is seriously suffering and full of anger towards the mother who does not immediately remove the pain. What use is that kind of mother? What use is that kind of God?

Experience of the loss of God makes us face these primitive expectations of him, unmasks the magician-god we harbour within us. It invites us also to meet the living God by being content to live within the muddle, the darkness, the suffering of life just as he came to live within it. It challenges us to know a God who deals with violence, cruelty, injustice, indifference by undergoing it, by taking into himself the God-less-ness of our fallen existence. It calls us to the heart of God, to live life as he lived it, to know it from within him. It's a call which offers us joy as well as sorrow within our bleakness and the prospect of sharing in his glory as we have shared in his grief. (Romans 6:5, 8, 17, 18; Philippians 3:7–11; 20, 21)

If we can stay with this intensely personal experience of God's absence and of encountering our false gods, we reach one of the great paradoxes of Christian life. At the point where we feel totally isolated, a thing of contempt to our fellow human-beings as well as to God, we find ourselves in a state encompassing the entire condition Jesus came to redeem. We can then begin to see some meaning in our feeling of having been asked to bear something greater than our own sin and weakness. We see that we have been drawn into experiencing the lost-ness of our race. We are enduring in ourselves what the Israelites underwent in the desert and in their Babylonian exile, re-enacting the drama, if you like, of fallen Man going back on his covenant with God and suffering the inevitable consequences. We then see that the Prodigal Son, eating his husks in a far-off land is each of us and all of us. When we feel our own misery we are being brought to share in the misery of all, in all ages. The poet Gerard Manley Hopkins, who knew so much about suffering of this kind, put it like this:

> *My cries heave, herds-long; huddle in a main, a*
> *chief —*
> *woe, world-sorrow; on an age-old anvil wince*
> *and sing.*[3]

In this state we learn 'feelingly' what we are: lost creatures helpless without their Creator and more, lost children hopeless without their Father. In the deepest part of ourselves we learn in a new way that we are made for God alone so that without him there is no rest, no fulfilment, no possibility of being 'at home' anywhere. We know where we are meant to be, with whom we are meant to be. 'The fall', 'original sin', 'alienation from God', all the concepts we have heard to explain our human condition in its wretchedness, take on a real significance for us. The need for reconciliation, for redemption, is one we now know with our whole being. The fate of the Godless is something we have begun to know from the inside. We have seen just what we amount to when left to our own illusions, memories, fantasies and pride. We know what it is to sit 'in darkness and the shadow of death' and wait for our redemption to come from the Lord. We are never alone in the darkness, in the desert: the whole of our race is there with us, in us.

Chapter 2

For God alone my soul waits in silence

For God alone my soul waits in silence;
from him comes my salvation.
He only is my rock and my salvation,
my fortress; I shall not be greatly moved.
(Psalm 62:1–2)

Most of us can probably remember a time when as children we were afraid of the dark; we feared the monsters hidden under the bed, perhaps, or the 'witch' that turned out to be the dressing gown hanging behind the door. The darkness made a familiar room and familiar things frightening, showing them to us through our fears and fantasies. It distorted external reality to reveal something of our inner imaginative or emotional life.

Even as adults it's at night, isn't it, that all our worries and fears tend to emerge full-blown? The darkness and emptiness of the night seem to offer us no refuge from them, provide no softening of the edges: everything seems stark and uncompromising. What the darkness tells us is often true, but incomplete; it is the truth of our lives when unsupported by rationality, by other people, by other aspects of our lives presently obscured by the blackness.

In our spiritual darkness we are much the same. At times God's absence, like the absence of light, leads us to see him through our fears and fantasies and we are like little children in the dark. At other times we are closer to our adult selves when left to our worries: the darkness leaves us no hiding-place from the knowledge of ourselves without God. The absence of light hides any access to reassurance we might once have gained from other people, from our ability to rationalize situations, from awareness of God's positive gifts to us. Our sinfulness and weakness appear starkly before us. It might be that we see how little capable of loving we are, how tainted are all our actions with self-regard (issuing from self-contempt as much as from self-love). It might be that long-buried resentments and hatreds emerge with all their venom. We may feel the full force of our jealousy, of our lust for power or acclaim, our egocentric and voracious desire for gratification of every kind. We may be brought face to face with our indifference and sloth, our desire to get through life with minimum disturbance and minimum emotional expenditure, our reluctance to commit ourselves to anyone or anything.

Normally we might have been shielded from too great a knowledge of these because awareness of God's presence threw a kindly light on us and our activities. Once this has gone only our vices show up in the darkness. We see only what is at enmity with God, what mars his image in us.

There is a twofold challenge here: to accept the truth it tells of our nothingness, our capacity for nothing but sin if left to our own devices; but also to accept that this is not however, the whole truth, because we are not abandoned children. There remains the hope of God's re-clothing us in *his* right-eousness; he has made us in his image, his desire is for us to recover its fullness. We are 'dust' but we are *his* dust: the darkness urges us to find all our hope, all our vision of man's glory in that fact of belonging to him and to wait in patience for him to gather us up and remould us.

For God alone

'You have made us for yourself, O God, and our hearts are restless until they find their rest in You.' These famous words of St. Augustine encapsulate the glory and the misery of being human; our wealth and our poverty. We are made for God, made to be moving towards him: this is the source of our human greatness, that our lives are not to be simply 'nasty, brutish and short' because they are intended for participation in God's life. But here, too, is the source of our misery: until we are fully and finally in relationship with him we are unfinished, at a loss to know what to do with ourselves. This is a state we detest. Our tendency is to prefer what is whole, complete and satisfyingly intact, what we would call perfect. This, surely, is the impulse behind all idol-worship, the desire to reduce what is beyond us to something not only visible and tangible but also gratifyingly complete and within bounds. Idolatry makes of our world a safe, closed, predictable system in which we need no longer endure our open-endedness, our rest-lessness, our seeking after something which moves on beyond us.

I think it is for this reason that the desert can

be such a powerful image in spiritual life. The emptiness, the vastness, the seeming endlessness of it defies our needs for recognizable boundaries, for assurance about the resources available to us. The desert means not only exposure to the elements, lack of necessities, isolation, not only the absence of familiar landmarks and the monotony of journeying through an unchanging, unyielding landscape. It also means experiencing mirage, experiencing the delusions and memories which we produce in defence against all these deprivations. The desert is the place for confronting illusion and idolatry.

This, of course, was exactly the discovery of the Israelites in the desert. Their rebellion there against God was a rejection of the unfinishedness, the open-endedness he was asking them to endure in exchanging the known demands of Egypt for an unseen Promised Land. It was a rebellion, like that of Adam and Eve in the book of Genesis, against their existence as creatures receiving their sustenance from the hand of God, in their wanting and valuing not what he gives in his time but what immediately gratifies their desires. How much better were the flesh-pots of Egypt to the boring diet of manna and quails! How much better to 'know where they stood' as slaves than be leading this wandering existence! The temptations they undergo test their faith and their acceptance of creatureliness, they test also their identity as the people of a God whose name 'I will be that I will be' defies our idolatrous instincts.

In our desert-place we do not, like the Israelites, build a golden calf but we do encounter the 'idols' we make to complete ourselves, to close us off to the pain and insecurity involved in waiting on an infinite God. We may discover, for example, how much we cling to spouse, parent, child, or friend, putting all our hope of affirmation and success onto them, whether it be by living through their achievements or by living only to please them, meeting their every expectation. We make of others, or allow them to be for us, objects meeting our need for adulation, affection, purpose, meaning.

It may be that our 'desert', our time 'without God' seems to intensify our ambition, in terms perhaps, of becoming 'someone to be reckoned with' in church or community life. We feel driven to escape this tremendous feeling of our own helplessness and uselessness by asserting our identity in the social world. We are tempted to make idols out of our 'self-development', to see ourselves as 'whole' people whose completeness blocks awareness of God as our final purpose. We may simply find ourselves desperate for affirmation from familiar or respected people, to give us something about ourselves to hold on to, like children cuddling their teddies in the night.

It's in this state that we so readily become attached to people, suffering the adult equivalent of the adolescent 'crush'. All our unmet longing for the infinite God, all our unfulfilled desire for assurance of his love, is transferred to a person who might meet our needs more immediately. And besides this, the sudden injection of feeling it brings provides a false impression of having recovered life and purpose. What relief from the bleak, flat facelessness of our inner landscape! You can imagine the sense of urgency, the excitement among the Israelites as they gathered together their gold for making the calf. At last something is happening, at last there's something for them to do!

When daily reality fails to offer a means of escape from our waiting on God, memory is often pressed into service. This, indeed, was the experience of the Israelites in their literal desert. Memory of the satisfaction of the most basic need, for food, overcomes awareness of the attendant circumstances, bondage. Recollection of variety and pleasure leads them to view the Egyptians with an unwarranted kindly eye.

It is the same for us. Memory softens and heightens aspects of events, making life before we let God in seem more fulfilling than it ever was or giving such a glow to our honeymoon period in prayer that it seems we have fallen from heaven. In this way memory diverts attention from our waiting on God in the emptiness of our desert into either nostalgic daydream or into useless lament for what used to be. Sometimes memories also emerge of past incidents we have long buried. Shame, pain, self-recrimination, self-pity are all aroused by these unexpected recollections. As long as our minds and feelings are occupied with these things from our past we do not feel the staleness and emptiness of the present. We find that we would sooner feel something, however grim, than nothing; sooner fight with monsters from the past than face doing nothing in the present; sooner see our lives painted in the lurid colours of guilt than endure the unrelieved greyness of daily living.

Memory also conspires in our flight from reality by encouraging us to gather up recollections of affirmation and of virtuous acts to stock ourselves up against the future, just as the Israelites were led to collect more than one day's supply of manna. For us, as for them, the effort is a failure and the harvest goes bad. When we have gathered in our little stock of virtues they crumble in our hands: we see them cracked and flawed with our own self-seeking or with our reliance on purely natural gifts of temperament which have, in truth, asked nothing of us.

The vastness of the desert, just like the darkness of the night, plays havoc with our perception. Our temptations are experienced magnified against the unrelieved expanse of the horizon, unsoftened by the outline of any growing, living thing. Their very starkness makes them more easily seen for what they are, makes *us* more easily seen for what we are. The desert strips us of our illusions of grandeur, of self-sufficiency, of self-righteousness. We realize how much of what we have considered as being 'spiritual' has been, in fact, a mere repression of our rebellious instincts or a desire to know God on our own terms. The idols we have made there fail to meet our true longings and we see just what they amount to – flight from ourselves, our emptiness, our fear of meaninglessness.

The desert invites us to deal with all this simply by accepting it, without shame, without self-justification, as the truth about ourselves, about us all, without God. Like Job we have to sit patiently on our dung-heap, calling for mercy, repenting by turning our whole selves towards the only One who can do something about it, refusing to collude with anything offering us false light, false hope, false refreshment. If we can wait patiently in this knowledge, then the smaller, the simpler we become, closer to that child-likeness whose only hope of glory lies in knowing and being known by a loving Father.

My soul waits

If we keep faith with this experience of God's absence we are sometimes left feeling we are locked in a hall of mirrors. Wherever we turn we seem to see distorted images of ourselves. The more we seem locked-in the less we feel capable of loving, of being able to reach beyond 'the prison-house of self'. Increasingly we come to feel that we are not so much in the desert or in the darkness, but that they are in us, are us. Previously we might have seen ourselves as, perhaps, an unweeded garden, messy but fertile. Now we feel more like derelict land, a rubbish tip. The house we had built for our inner selves to inhabit, our self-image, has fallen into ruins. Where we may have felt that we were, at least, a passable product of God the potter now we feel like one of his rejects, broken and cast aside in the corner.

Furthermore, we cannot do all those cheery things we have been advised to do. We can't walk towards any speck of light because we are all darkness, we feel as unable to move from our rubbish-dump or hovel as the Israelites were to leave the desert. We can't 'look on the bright side' because there is none; there is, however, a curious awareness that, painful though the state is, we must not flee it, even if we could.

So the darkness and the dryness teach us to wait on God's mercy and on his timing, acknowledging that our idolatry, our obsessions, our flight, have got us nowhere. We realize that we cannot and do not save ourselves, that by ourselves we cannot rebuild our ruin or reclaim our waste-land. Only God can do it, when he will.

This waiting, although it seems to make us very passive is, in fact, a very active time. Our being content to wait in poverty and uselessness is our withdrawal of consent to our basic sinfulness, that is, the desire for our will to become God's will and for our lives to be our possession. Waiting starves the root of that sin in us, saying to the Lord, 'What You will, in the way You will it to be, when You will and for as long as You will it to be.' It is signing the blank sheet of paper on which God writes the terms of our relationship with him. It is reversing the original 'no' to God of Adam and Eve when, in taking the fruit, they took themselves out of God's hands, out of dependence on his timing and judgement of their needs and declared themselves independent beings. Waiting makes us one with Jesus in his great 'yes' to the Father in Gethsemane.

My soul waits in silence

Silence may seem a contradictory term to use about this state. God, indeed, no longer 'speaks' but the emptiness has soon been filled with the internal clamour of our desires, obsessions, fears and idolatries. This desert at night is a noisy place.

This is one of its great temptations: we can become so preoccupied with the inner turmoil that we may lose awareness of the silence beneath it, the longing for God who, as far as we are concerned, has abandoned us, or, to change the image, we become so transfixed by the extent of our delapidation that we forget to look out beyond our tumbledown walls to watch for the builder's arrival.

The noise, the ruin, must be recognized but must not occupy centre stage. All our attention needs to be directed towards the coming of the One who stills the storms and rebuilds the Temple. We need to sit firmly within our chaos, looking upward and out-ward towards the horizon, however empty it appears. In this way the desert can lead us into the fullness of hope, in this combination of a firm rooting in present reality, however grim, and a trusting expectation that, despite all appearance to the contrary, God cannot, and will not, fail us.

The more we learn simply to be content to be this rubbish-tip from which we look for the Lord, the more we are attentive to his silence amid our noise, the more we find that our unruly clamour is eased back from its central position and that, although still a powerful force, it no longer preoccupies our mind, feelings and conscience. It does not usurp God's place within us. And so, while aridity, darkness, helplessness remain we find at the core of this experience a spaciousness which speaks of preparation for new life rather than of death. The emptiness caused by devastation and loss has the chance to become also the 'humble space' in which the Lord, in his own time, can come to birth in us. What we may have known as a piece of abstract doctrine becomes something we live: salvation isn't completed yet, the seeds are sown but the harvest is still to come; we are caught in the tension between what God has already done for us in Christ and its coming to fruition. The space being created in us through our waiting on God is the place where creation is in travail, bringing the sons of God to birth. Our struggle against the sense of futility and emptiness, our sense of imprisonment in a hall of mirrors of self, is part and parcel of the working-out of the Redemption as St. Paul describes it in Romans 8:

For the creation waits with eager longing for the revealing of the sons of God; for the creation was subjected to futility, not of its own will but by the will of him who subjected it in hope; because the creation itself will be set free from its bondage to decay and obtain the glorious liberty of the children of God. We know that the whole creation has been groaning in travail together until now; and not only the creation, but we ourselves, who have the first fruits of the Spirit, groan inwardly as we wait for adoption as sons, the redemption of our bodies. For in this hope we were saved. Now hope that is seen is not hope. For who hopes for what he sees? But if we hope for what we do not see, we wait for it with patience.
(Romans 8:19–25)

Vaguely we may glimpse a possibility that what is happening to us is not so much an affliction but an expression of our Christian calling to be looking for the coming of the Lord, hastening the coming of the Kingdom by giving ourselves as territory from which it may advance.

Much of the time we lose grasp of this wider context for our aridity and bleakness. All too often the vision of our own awfulness seems to block out all other perceptions; then, far from waiting in silence we fall into self-rejecting lament. At other times we are seduced into minimizing our responsibility for our state: we grumble about God or get entangled in the coils of self-justification. Gradually, however, as we learn to establish just a pin-point of attention beneath the inner clamour and distress, in which hope can take root, we begin to wait in silence, that is, without resentful complaint against God, self or others. We may still need to voice our pain, to register the oppressiveness of the bleakness within but we are no longer full of protest because we are beginning to accept that this is part of God's purpose for us. What happens to us in the process doesn't matter, finally: we may not like it, we may wish he had other ways of going about things, but if this is his choice, so be it. We may never attain it but we see that what is asked of us is that utter self-abandonment in love epitomized by the prayer of Charles de Foucauld:

Father, I abandon myself into your hands,
Do with me what you will,
Whatever You may do, I thank You.
I am ready for all, I accept all.
Let only Your will be done in me
And in all Your creatures,

I ask no more than this, O Lord.
Into Your hands I commit my soul.
I give it to you with all the love of my heart,
For I love You, Father,
And so need to give myself,
To abandon myself
Without reserve and with boundless confidence,
For You are my Father.[1]

And we recognize, with Charles de Foucauld, that this is Jesus' prayer to the Father, that only he can truly say it. In this recognition we are moved more deeply into silence for we realize that in the end Jesus must speak for us to the Father. What matters for us then, in our desert, is not to bother ourselves with ourselves but to keep our sight resolutely on the person of Jesus, especially in his desolation, forgetting ourselves in remembering him.

So the desert simplifies us. It cuts away our self-concern, after first, perhaps, blowing it up beyond proportion. It cuts down the defences of fine words and thoughts we had hidden behind; it cuts off our escape route from God. It destroys our hope of a salvation coming from anyone or anything but God. It makes us 'single issue' people for whom only the coming of the Kingdom matters.

Our prayer is simplified, too, into the one plea for mercy, however we may express it. We may not be conscious of any feeling towards God; there may be nothing more than a very bare awareness that we both need and want him as the God of our life, even though he seems to have forgotten us or we seem incapable of responding to him. Praying then becomes, essentially, simply living with this awareness and not only in set times when we do nothing but sit and want him. Prayer at this time is more than ever about our disposition and not about what we do. We have to be like the poorest beggar, setting out with his bowl into the deserted street in the middle of the night to ensure he misses no-one in the morning. The beggar's only asset is his destitution which he must not hide. He must endure the absurdity of waiting in darkness, on

empty streets, if he is to ensure a meeting with someone who will fill his bowl. This is our prayer: to make our inner being as available, as exposed, as vulnerable as possible while we wait for him to show himself in our lives. Like the beggar we must endure the sense of absurdity accompanying this vigilance. We have to spend day after day waiting for the One who can restore a sense of meaning to our lives, without being fully sure who he is and what will become of us.

This state makes our prayer very honest. We have to come to times of prayer acknowledging to God and to ourselves that we feel it is useless, that we would rather do anything than pray or rather, that we would rather do anything than this poor excuse for prayer. It seems as though we are talking to ourselves as we disclose our doubts about the sanity of praying to an absent God but in persevering we offer him the prayer of pure faith. When we have 'got off our chests' our immediate responses all we can then do is still ourselves and wait, making space within by refusing to listen to our thoughts, perhaps by using a word or phrase which focuses us entirely on God. For some people this may be the Jesus Prayer (Lord Jesus Christ, Son of the Living God, have mercy on me, a sinner) or the name of Jesus; for others it will be a phrase from a psalm or a favourite text which sums up this intentness upon God. At times it may simply be a word like 'Yes', yes to the absurdity and the waiting, yes to whatever he is doing with us. It will be a 'Yes' which recognizes our fears, our hesitations and our desire to say 'No' or 'Not yet', lays these bare within us and puts our weight, our choice, on that part of us, however fragile, which opts for God. All we can do in our prayer is offer him our good will, puny and feeble though it is, and let him do the rest. We may hanker after doing something stimulating in prayer, something which makes us feel that the enterprise is worthwhile. This sort of prayer may seem as empty, as dry, as flat as the rest of our inner world. We have to learn to give the Lord what he wants of us, our will, and not what we want to give him. We have to learn, over and over again, the truth of St. John of the Cross' counsel:

When you want to have everything,
Go where you have nothing.
When you want to be everything,
Go where you are nothing.[2]

This is where God wants us to be: our job in prayer is to ensure that we stay there until he chooses otherwise.

Chapter 3

Strategies for survival

This is my comfort in my affliction
that thy promise gives me life ...
Thy statutes have been my songs
in the house of my pilgrimage.
I remember thy name in the night, O Lord,
and keep thy law.

(Psalm 119:50, 54, 55)

The Israelites in the desert were a travelling people. However over-used it may be, I think the idea of the Christian life as a journey or pilgrimage to God has within it both a truth to our roots and to our experience of growth and change. One important point for any traveller is attainment of a balance between taking too much or too little for the journey. If we are encumbered with useless, oppressively heavy baggage the going becomes tough and slow. If we set out without any preparation at all, without resources and consideration of the demands of the journey, we may well come to grief at the first major, unforeseen difficulty.

The literal truth of this was impressed on me some years ago, when I was part of a group staying in the Peak District. On a day when we were going walking I had risen and breakfasted long before the others, according to my normal habit. The weather was bad. It had snowed heavily. A lot of energy went into keeping warm and ploughing through deep drifts. By lunch-time I was more than ready for food; by my personal clock it was nearer tea-time – and perilously close to the limits of my endurance. Then we discovered there was no food, each rucksack-wearer believing it was being carried in the other's bag. So began my first (and I hope, last) experience of exposure, in what seemed a desert of snow. Everywhere looked the same; the snow levelled all landmarks so that my addled brain lost what little sense of direction it normally possessed. I could only stumble blindly after others, scarcely able to keep on my feet. Wherever I fell I would lie there laughing, unaware of cold and wet. This hysteria alternated with phases of intense despair. It was my worst nightmare come true – nothing within for sustenance and nothing but vast, monochrome emptiness outside. On my own I could not have survived.

Looking back, I see now how much there is to learn from this about travelling through spiritual desert places: we must know our limits and needs, we must have some form of food for the journey, we must not travel entirely alone.

The first big mistake in the Peaks was my proud reliance on my own way of doing things, and my conviction that I was strong enough to manage on the little food and sleep I'd allowed myself. I had refused to submit to the realities of the new situation.

It's the same spiritually. We refuse to recognize our weakness and become convinced in 'good' times that our faith is strong enough to survive any trial. We do not realize that much of this 'faith' is padded-out with feelings and wishful thinking; it's enough for our everyday circumstances, just as a 5 a.m. start on a winter's day was feasible in my normally sedentary life in a warm house. So often we don't realize that we are already pushing ourselves to the limits of our natural resources, materially, physically and spiritually. Any new demand then produces a real 'exposure' of our frailty. We have not acquired, as part of ourselves, the outlook which enables us to withstand spiritual drought or famine, just as I had not built up the stamina and the physical resources for my hike.

As Christians I think we perhaps need to accept that we are always on a route to God which may pass through the desert: we dare not live on starvation rations. By this I mean that we need to be feeding continually on truth, on doctrine, so that we are not living solely according to *our* feelings, *our* choices, *our* way of understanding the Gospel.

For some of us this may involve concentrating our attention on the basic truths about God as Creator, Father, Redeemer, Lover, especially emphasizing, perhaps, those which we find most difficult emotionally. The need is to allow God to be greater than our powerful feelings. For me, at stages in my life when psychological and emotional difficulties have been uppermost, this has been a matter of directing reading, thinking and praying, towards this one aspect of God in an openness of mind and heart which consents, as it were, to its truth. When we have such difficulties we can often find that beneath it is a powerful resistance to the idea: we don't like God as Creator, because we don't like the implications of being a creature; we can't accept God as 'Father' because we take a dim view of fathers.

During one period of darkness, for example, I

discovered that God's 'absence' resulted from an unwillingness to let God love me, to let God be Love. I couldn't cope with a gift I hadn't earned because it was humiliating, belittling. For me the message behind being loved was about my worthlessness, my incapacity to give anything of value. To be loved unconditionally was, for me, to be deprived of any human dignity. Once I realized this I realized that there was also a gap between my mind and my feelings. Intellectually I saw that this idea was wrong-headed and distorted, while emotionally I still 'knew' it was true. No amount of argument or persuasion had any power in this situation: it was my feelings which needed re-educating. So I immersed myself as far as possible in brooding upon God as Love – in Scripture, in accounts of Christian experience, in my own life – in a willingness to surrender my own view of love. And in prayer I could only ask him to teach me his meaning of love and offer him a willingness to learn afresh. Certainly I have found again and again that our only way through this kind of impasse is to foster within us some readiness, however faltering, to surrender to God our often cherished and distorted ideas and images, by meditating on his truth in a way which says, 'Lord, I want to believe this, I want to know it with the whole of my being. I don't want to be stuck in myself and my reactions. Teach me what it means.'

For those of us whose difficulties lie more in the area of intellectual doubt, the need is to allow God to be bigger than our minds and our theories, but the approach is the same. Our study and thinking needs to take place in the desire 'to have the mind of Christ' rather than to conform him to our opinions.

My personal motto is an ancient one 'I believe in order to understand', which I take to mean living in openness to the truth I am struggling with. This is difficult to explain as it is so much a matter of being rather than of doing. But take, for example, the doctrine of the Trinity. Intellectually I find this a very strange notion and I could easily be side-tracked into arguments about Neo-Platonism and its 'infection' of Christianity. Instead I choose to be open to the church's teaching about the Trinity and allow myself the possibility of knowing God in this way. Living in this kind of trust makes one docile to, and teachable by, the Holy Spirit so that gradually what is read and pondered about the doctrine comes to make more sense. The position one takes up is that God should be allowed to expand our intellect instead of our intellect being allowed to reduce God to its proportions.

This kind of faith which transcends our individual preferences and quirks is our chief resource for the journey. To help us it has to be part of us, part of our habitual way of experiencing life rather than something taken along as an extra package. On my literal journey I could have endured the absence of food had I not started it already on the edge of hunger. This is how we are in the desert. We discover that we are without external resources – the support of our feelings and the sense of God's presence; all that is left to us is the capacity for a faith which can withstand being contradicted by experience.

This kind of faith is nourished by memory in its positive aspects. We need to reject the false memory which leads to idolatry, but we need also to develop a habitual memory of all that God has done for us.

Our faith rests on this capacity for recollection of the Lord's great acts of salvation: the Exodus, the return from Babylonian exile, the Cross and Resurrection. Our Eucharist is a 'bringing to mind' not only of a past event but of the ever-present saving action of God. Remembering what the Lord has done is also, always, remembering what he does now and will do. He is the God of the living, the Eternal One into whom past, present and future are gathered.

We need to cultivate this habit of positive mindfulness of God's activity to counter the power of negative memory. This tells us that the past held all our hope of salvation, that getting back to what we once had or were is the only way to achieve 'the good life'. Positive memory helps us to ground our hope wholly in the fidelity of God, who was, is and always will be, Love. It provides our resource in the desert, an underpinning conviction that the God who led us in green pastures and by still waters is the same God who is working out our salvation in the rocky, dry places of our lives.

What we take on our journey in the desert, or by night, must be part of ourselves, as stamina and a fit body should have been mine in the Peak District. Our 'survival kit' is a capacity to live in mindfulness of what we know and believe about our God, aided by the associated habit of holding our feelings and opinions at arm's length from our 'hearts', our place of relationship with God. These make us poor in ourselves, receptive to what is offered us rather than stocked-up with our own ideas and abilities: our great resource in the desert is nothing to do with *our* capacities at all, it is all to do with our conviction about God's unfailing capacity for loving and saving us.

And there is, of course, a third provision for our journey, one which may seem far too insubstantial to be of any use but is, indeed, the most important element for our survival – our desire for God, our desire to belong to him, to see him face to face.

Our resources for the desert journey are beginning to look familiar, aren't they? Faith, mindfulness, which lays the ground for hope, and desire for God, the precursor of love. Of course, if we had these in abundance our journey would be unnecessary, superfluous. In fact, they are usually quite small seeds in us or tiny plants easily squashed by our capacity for self-love, illusion and cowardice. They seem very fragile resources on which to rely, but it is this very fragility which ultimately proves their strength. They are enough only to throw us entirely on God for our sustenance, without any risk that we might rest in the gifts of God rather than in him as the giver. We cannot lay claim to salvation on account of our faith, hope and love but only on account of the need they have exposed within us. For myself, my 'survival kit' boils down to the advice Walter Hilton, a fourteenth-century spiritual guide, gave to the pilgrims on their spiritual journey to Jerusalem, that is, to Jesus:

> *Repeat, 'I am nothing, I have nothing, I neither seek nor desire anything but the love of Jesus'.*[1]

Your statutes have been my songs

For some of us, just one sentence which sums up our faith, hope and love is all that is needed to provide support and direction on our journey. I suppose for many it may be the words of the Jesus prayer: 'Lord Jesus Christ, Son of the living God, have mercy on me, a sinner.' For others, something more individually-wrought or more extended is of greater help. We may need to garner our own collection of Bible verses and words of guidance which keep our hearts and minds directed Godwards, focused on his truth.

It may help to cull the Psalms and to learn by

heart those verses which most reflect the desolation
we feel and our confidence in the faithfulness of God.
Whenever I feel in exile I would naturally turn to
Psalm 42:

As a hart longs for flowing streams,
so longs my soul for thee, O God.
My soul thirsts for God, for the living God.
When shall I come and behold the face of God?
My tears have been my food day and night,
while men say to me continually, 'Where is
your God?'

(vv 1–3)

and to the opening verse of Psalm 63:

O God, thou art my God, I seek thee,
my soul thirsts for thee;
my flesh faints for thee,
as in a dry and weary land where no water is.

When I'm in danger of being overwhelmed by the
need to grumble and by a forgetfulness of God's
mercies I turn to a psalm which seems to do the
same, such as Psalm 77:

I cry aloud to God,
aloud to God, that he may hear me.
In the day of my trouble I seek the Lord;
in the night my hand is stretched
out without wearying; . . .

. . . I meditate and search my spirit:
'Will the Lord spurn for ever;
and never again be favourable?
Has his steadfast love for ever ceased?

Are his promises at an end for all time?
Has God forgotten to be gracious? . . .'

. . . I will call to mind the deeds of the Lord;
yea, I will remember thy wonders of old.
I will meditate on all thy work,
and muse on thy mighty deeds.
(vv 1–2, 6–9, 11–12)

and to those verses which offer reassurance:

My soul makes its boast in the Lord;
let the afflicted hear and be glad.

. . . I sought the Lord, and he answered me,
and delivered me from all my fears.

. . . This poor man cried, and the Lord heard
him, and saved him out of all his troubles.
(Psalm 34:2, 4, 6)

Perhaps the lines I use most as my lifebelt in times
of desperation come from Psalm 142:

I cry to thee, O Lord;
I say, Thou art my refuge,
my portion in the land of the living.
Give heed to my cry;
for I am brought very low!

(vv 5–6)

Indeed, the whole Psalm offers, for me, that balance between praise and confidence in God, and
expression of personal pain which keeps the latter

in perspective. There are many others, the penitential Psalms,[2] for example, and those which celebrate God's power to save. Perhaps the best-known and and best-loved penitential Psalm is Psalm 51, with its combination of sorrow for sin and deep trust in a forgiving and restoring God:

Have mercy on me, O God,
according to thy steadfast love;
according to thy abundant mercy blot out my
transgressions,
Wash me thoroughly from my iniquity,
and cleanse me from my sin! . . .

. . . Purge me with hyssop, and I shall be clean;
wash me, and I shall be whiter than snow.
Fill me with joy and gladness;
let the bones which thou hast broken rejoice.
Hide thy face from my sins,
and blot out all my iniquities.

Create in me a clean heart, O God,
and put a new and right spirit within me.
. . . Restore to me the joy of thy salvation,
and uphold me with a willing spirit . . .
. . . O Lord, open thou my lips,
and my mouth shall show forth thy praise.
For thou hast no delight in sacrifice;
were I to give a burnt offering, thou wouldst not
be pleased.
The sacrifice acceptable to God is a broken
  spirit;
a broken and contrite heart, O God, thou wilt
  not despise.

(vv 1–2, 7–12, 15–17)

Trust and patient assurance of God's goodness are also the keynotes of the penitence found in Psalm 130:

I wait for the Lord, my soul waits,
and in his word I hope;
my soul waits for the Lord
more than watchmen for the morning,
more than watchmen for the morning.
O Israel, hope in the Lord!
For with the Lord there is steadfast love,
and with him is plenteous redemption.
And he will redeem Israel from all his iniquities.
                                    (vv 5–8)

These cannot, in our state, alter our feelings, but they do nourish our faith, giving us expressions of confidence and hope to occupy our fretted hearts and minds which enable us to keep self-pity, fear and doubt from taking possession of them.

For similar nourishment I turn habitually in dry times to the promises of salvation in Isaiah and Ezekiel, with a will to believe in the new life they herald. When my trust in God is shaky and I am tempted to wonder just what kind of God he amounts to, I love to counter it with favourite verses from Ezekiel 34:

I, I myself will search for my sheep,
and will seek them out, . . . I will seek
the lost, and I will bring back the
strayed, and I will bind up the crippled,
and I will strengthen the weak, and the fat
and the strong I will watch over; I will
feed them in justice.

                                    (vv 11, 16)

When it is myself, rather than God, that I question, when I feel more like a rejected 'second' than a genuine human-being, it is Ezekiel who offers an anchor. He prevents me from looking to myself for salvation, for virtues or abilities which might mitigate the sense of helplessness. I am thinking particularly of the vision of the Valley of Dry Bones (Ezekiel 37:1–14) and the great promise in the preceding chapter:

> *I will sprinkle clean water upon you, and you*
> *shall be clean from all your uncleannesses, and*
> *from all your idols I will cleanse you. A new*
> *heart I will give you, and a new spirit I will put*
> *within you; and I will take out of your flesh the*
> *heart of stone and give you a heart of flesh.*
> *(Ezekiel 36:25–26)*

And Isaiah, too, provides that same hope for the poor, the dried-up, the helpless:

> *Ho, everyone who thirsts,*
> *come to the waters;*
> *and he who has no money,*
> *come, buy and eat!*
> *Come, buy wine and milk*
> *without money and without price.*
> *(Isaiah 55:1, 2)*

and for those whose only hope is in God's mercy:

> *I dwell in the high and holy place,*
> *and also with him who is of a contrite and*
> *humble spirit,*

to revive the spirit of the humble,
and to revive the heart of the contrite.
For I will not contend for ever,
nor will I always be angry.

(Isaiah 57:15, 16)

It is not only that these words speak to my condition now which gives me perspective on my aridity, it is the knowledge that these prayers and promises have also nourished many Christians and Jews before me, that they express something of the human search for God. In some way this lessens, for me, the sense of isolation which can be so oppressive.

When we are feeling faith-less, hope-less, love-less, to turn mentally to our own special passages will not alter our feelings but it will affirm our desire to set God's promises and mercy at the centre of our lives.

Praying and living the Psalms and the prophets in this way also brings us close to Jesus: these are the Scriptures which nourished him, which shaped his abandonment to the Father. Looking at him directly in the Gospel also anchors us in hope: Jesus choosing the rash and thoughtless Peter; Jesus sitting at table with sinners; Jesus refusing to join in public condemnations; Jesus calming the storm. Each is a promise for us.

But perhaps most of all we need to look at Jesus in his passion. This can be difficult for some of us because the initial association here is not with consolation but with guilt. Too frequently in the past we were taught to look at the cross and say, 'I did that'. The cross then seems more concerned with our sinfulness than with God's goodness. In other traditions, or at other times, God's great love shown in the cross has, indeed, been stressed but in such a way that our failure to respond is maximized, creating a different kind of guilt.

Both approaches have their place but neither reaches the heart of the cross, which is simply God being himself, giving himself in such a way that nothing can come between him and the creatures he loves. All that is ours is now God's. The horror of God-less-ness is now known by the one who, because he is a true son, can know it more fully than anyone else. The cross makes Jesus the place, as it were, in which all experience of estrangement now occurs. However far we fall, however dry our desert, however black our night, the depths, the aridity, the darkness now belongs to Christ. *Nothing* in our experience now has the power to separate us from the love of God:

> *For I am sure that neither death, nor life, nor angels, nor principalities, nor things present, nor things to come, nor powers, nor height, nor depth, nor anything else in all creation, will be able to separate us from the love of God in Christ Jesus our Lord.*
>
> *(Romans 8:38, 39)*

Our ultimate support in the desert lies in this conviction, which may cut across all our feelings: God is truly he 'in whom we live and move and have our being' whether in darkness or light, famine or plenty, aridity or growth.

Meditating on Jesus in his passion, like our feeding on the Old Testament, meets our need to avoid isolation in our journey. In one sense, we *are* uniquely and intensely alone in this desert-place: God deprives us of any hiding-place in other people. In another, as I have already suggested, we are being brought into the deepest experiences of the human race in its quest for God. As we contemplate the sufferings of Jesus we remember that all of us find the meaning of our anguish there, that our desolation is set within the context of the desolation and redemption of our

race. We realize the truth of St. Paul's words: 'as in Adam all die, so also in Christ shall all be made alive.' (1 Corinthians 15:20) We come to a true sense of ourselves as members of a pilgrim people.

If we come to this realization of our belonging to a people, we lose another set of blinkers put on us, at times by our pride, at times by our immersion in our pain. We have hitherto felt we were in this alone, left to carry the burden of our dereliction by ourselves. Now we begin to see that what has been helping to keep the shreds of faith, hope and love alive in us has been the prayer, faith, hope and love of our fellow Christians. We are not only travelling with other people, we are also at times being carried by them.

Your statutes have been my songs in the house of my pilgrimage

When our time of darkness and aridity has been very long and intense we may feel that we have nothing left. Our faith seems reduced to a mere point of dry, stubborn conviction set amidst a mass of clamouring objections and doubts. Our hope seems like a refusal to accept reality; our love seems non-existent.

If we look at ourselves closely we find that all we have left is our will, our capacity to choose. The desert reduces the Gospel to one bald statement which offers little comfort to our feelings and imagination: 'If you love me, you will keep my commandments.' (John 14:15) It invites us to prove our love, that is, our choice of God, by doing all that is asked of us regardless of our feelings. It pushes us to accept what we may most rebel against – that true love means obedience. If we do accept it, it will lead us not only to maintaining our now-repugnant pattern of prayer and reading but also to fulfilling conscientiously all the requirements of love in our daily lives, regardless of the absence of any spontaneity. This brings with it the readiness to feel hypocritical because of this lack of fit between our actions and our disposition. It goes hard with us when we have suffered in the loss of our illusions and pretensions to be back with this apparent inauthenticity. It goes even harder for us if we have been led to believe that our growth as Christians would lead to a continuous development of spontaneity. What we have overlooked is the fact that, as can never be repeated too often, union with God is in the first place union of our will with his. It is only when we will as he wills that we can be truly spontaneous, because he will be the fountain of life within us. Before this so much of what we have called immediacy has been an outpouring from our own personality which has little direct connection with our spiritual state.

These earlier experiences of 'overflowing' love for God or neighbour are enjoyable, making us feel expanded, exalted, in tune with the world. They bring their immediate reward, which may spur us on spiritually but they can also seduce us into preferring the feelings they bring, to God as source of love. Darkness and dryness teach us, as I've already suggested, a love in which there is no discernible reward. We *choose* the loving act, in spite of our inclinations, because this is God's way and we prefer his way to ours. We choose it despite the absence of any sense of fulfilment, despite the pain it brings in acknowledging that nothing we may do can earn the presence of God. We have to go on 'pleasing God' by keeping his commandments without any reference to what it does or does not do for us.

An example of this kind of selfless love of God which I cherish is from the life of St. Francis de Sales. As a young Catholic student, Francis was wrestling with the doctrine of predestination. He went into a period of extreme spiritual anguish, of complete darkness in which he became convinced of his damnation. Instead of surrendering to despair however, Francis made his choice of God and wrote out a solemn declaration to God of his intention of serving him even in hell. We can give the Lord nothing greater than this determination that he will be our God even if we were to lose him forever. (It is, of course, a logical impossibility, for God cannot be truly absent where there is such love, but what have love and logic to do with one another?)

This is an immensely painful condition but it does bring peace in the darkness because we know, in some obscure way, that God *is* and that everything important is contained in that bare fact. This knowledge persists, dimly, no matter how much we feel that heaven is a dream or is eternally barred to us. Humanly speaking we don't like what is happening to us, we would still prefer to feel all those things which previously comforted us but somehow we know that we are what and how we have to be. We know there is truth for us in Dante's words, 'In His will is our peace'.

Chapter 4

Kept as the apple of his eye

*He found him in a desert land, and in the
howling waste of the wilderness;
he encircled him, he cared for him,
he kept him as the apple of his eye.*
                              (Deuteronomy 32:10)

'In His will is our peace.' These words from Dante's
Divine Comedy sum up his vision after journeying
through hell to heaven; they equally well might sum
up the message of this book. After the experience
of lostness, of waiting and of suffering the consequences of being oneself, comes the experience of joy,
of heaven, of God. After the suffering of incarnate
life, after the cross, after the descent into hell, there
is resurrection and return to the Father in glory.

How easy it is to lose or ignore this wholeness
about Christian living! By and large our more recent
forebears were too possessed by the suffering Jesus,
to have much to say about the glorified Lord. Now
we, in the usual pendulum swing, seem in danger
of having nothing positive to say about suffering
and of relegating the cross to the status of one of
God's possible options for Jesus. In a 'fun culture'
the pressure is on us to put all our emphasis upon
celebration of eternal life as *here and now*: the for-
mer 'vale of tears' of this life has now to become an

endless party. These are our extremes; by painting them in their boldest colours perhaps we may see them more clearly.

When our life with God is more or less life without God, when it is arid and bleak, a grasp of the wholeness of the Christian vision, of cross leading to resurrection, of suffering giving way to joy, is vital. Otherwise we sink into a belief in a God of suffering or we label all our pain as bad and try to get out of it by any available means.

Today it is the latter temptation which proves more seductive, I suspect, and it frequently leads us into denying the reality either of our darkness or of our relationship with God. Haven't we all, at some time, met good Christians whose suffering in times of God's absence has been intensified by their conviction that this shouldn't be happening at all? I know I have. I try to assure them that pain in our spiritual life serves the same purposes as in our physical life. It may tell us that something is wrong and needs healing but it may also tell us that the process is already under way. It shows us what is at odds with God within us in a way which is itself a sign of hope: it affirms that we *do* want God, that we do not feel perfectly well without him. It is only the diseased nervous system which registers no pain. The continuance of pain is likewise so often the sign to us that a healing process is hidden within the darkness: what is opposed to him is being confronted and driven out while the 'bones' of our distorted relationship are being re-set in their proper position.

If we can accept this we can learn, at one level, to love our time of darkness because we know that in it and through it God is making us more like himself and ready to see him face to face. It is not a process in which we can see clearly what the Lord is doing with us. He is laying in store for us the gift of our identity which we shall know only when all darkness is past. Remember the words of St. John:

> *We are God's children now; it does not yet appear what we shall be, but we know that when he appears we shall be like him, for we shall see him as he is. And every one who thus hopes in him purifies himself as he is pure.*
>
> *(1 John 3:2–3)*

Only we realize now that it is not so much our 'purifying ourselves' which matters as allowing him to achieve it in us.

Accepting this we can then learn to pray the Psalms of affliction which have previously consoled us with greater serenity because we know that all that happens to us is an aspect of God's jealous love for us. As T.S. Eliot suggested, he is acting as surgeon in our lives so that only those things in us which live for him survive and grow. If this leaves us feeling very maimed, very little, very vulnerable, very poor, then so much the better for we know that these are the qualities he allowed in his Son, the qualities which attract his mercy.

After reading this I find myself arguing with myself. 'What about the darkness which comes from my infidelity, my moodiness, my depression? Surely I can't love that time, too?' And I have to answer myself with what I really know already, that I must love it if it deprives me of reliance on myself. I have to remind myself that God is a superbly economical housewife who never wastes anything. Any experience of ours he can use for our good if only we are humble enough to let him. We are held 'in the palm of his hand' so that our falls, though they seem to be on hard and rocky ground or into an endless chasm, are only taking us more deeply into the abyss of his mercy. Whatever the source of our darkness and dryness we can love it as the means God uses to make us his own, just as Jesus loved, and embraced the cross, the end result of man's folly and rebellion, as the means to make all humankind his own. We, like him, can have no love for the pain in itself, but we accept it willingly for love of its purpose.

In the days of his flesh, Jesus offered up prayers and supplications, with loud cries and tears (Hebrews 5:7)

Darkness, bleakness, apparent loss of God may bring about our personal healing and in it we come to know our part in bearing the burden of our race. But these individual experiences cannot be understood fully if we look at them outside the experience of Christ. The 'cross' we bear must be seen in the light of Jesus' cross. We cannot explore and understand, we cannot 'get to the bottom of' our experience of dereliction unless we immerse ourselves in contemplation of Jesus' living out of our God-less-ness. Surrendering to the Father in our desolation, as Jesus did in his, not only purifies us, more importantly it draws us into his saving work, and makes us intercessors and co-workers with Christ. In our own small way he brings us to say with St. Paul:

*Now I rejoice in my sufferings for your sake,
and in my flesh I complete what is lacking in
Christ's afflictions for the sake of his body, that
is, the church.*

(Colossians 1:24)

So, for the fullest perspective on our 'dry land' we need to look at Jesus in his dry places, in the desert and on the cross.

We have seen how the need to wait on God brings us to the roots of our sinfulness; we want to be like God on *our* terms, according to our timing, possessing and controlling our existence. Waiting shows up the 'old man', Adam, in us. It shows up too, our likeness to the Israelites in the desert. They made a god for themselves, to fulfil their own purposes, when they had tired of God who was fashioning them for *his* purposes. Waiting exposes our rebellion but it calls us also to union with the One who said a final 'No' to the temptations of the Old Man, bringing a possibility of new life.

In his desert experience Jesus is tempted, like Adam and Eve, to take his life out of his Father's hands into his own; to refuse the Father's timing; to exchange the fullness of participation in the Father's life for immediate power, for the illusion of control. All the temptations – to turn stones into bread, to leap from the parapet of the Temple, to worship Satan in return for power, are temptations to pre-empt God's timing and to conform his ways to man's. Adam and Eve, the Israelites in the desert and Jesus, each have a choice: wait on God's will to satisfy your needs and desires, or use the powers he has given you to have something for yourself now, something gratifyingly yours and gratifyingly immediate.

Leaping from the Temple parapet is characteristic of the way we parody God's ways so that we can pre-empt his action in us. How much more tempting it is to 'sacrifice' ourselves showily when it isn't asked of us, to prove our closeness to God, than to wait for him to bring us into more costly, less glorious and less glamorous self-oblation. And it's a parody, more than anything, of God's choice of the cross. When he is hungry, thirsty, without consolation, Jesus is tempted to act upon his understanding of sacrifice and resurrection in purely human terms, in order to prove his sonship and to have factual evidence about himself and his Father's love, to which he can cling.

Turning stones into bread, like taking the fruit and like complaining about manna in the desert, is not only about meeting immediate appetite it's also about our desire for independence. We hate having to accept what we're given. We want to look after ourselves, be our own boss, using our powers to get what we want when we want it. We have no wish to remain creatures, receiving sustenance from God's hand, living according to his will and not ours. Stones turned into bread would satisfy not only physical appetite for food but psychological appetite for self-sufficiency.

God promises to make us 'first-born sons' (Hebrews 12:23); we are 'co-heirs with Christ' (Romans 8:17). Wonderful – but there is one snag. It is a promise for the future, an heir does not possess his estate now. We must endure the sufferings of this present time for the sake of future glory:

When we cry, 'Abba! Father!' it is the Spirit himself bearing witness with our spirit that we are children of God, and if children, then heirs, heirs of God and fellow heirs with Christ, provided we suffer with him in order that we may also be glorified with him.

I consider that the sufferings of this present time are not worth comparing with the glory that is to be revealed to us.

(Romans 8:15b–18)

The temptation to worship Satan in return for an immediate reign over the world meets us in our reluctance to wait, in our desire to be 'as gods' here and now. It appeals to the strain of materialism in our thinking – better the one bird in the hand of this-worldly dominance than the two birds in the bush of sharing in God's glory. Who knows whether God will keep his promise? Maybe it's all pie in the sky to keep us subservient. Giving allegiance to what is not God for the sake of immediate fulfilment is to be like Eve in heeding the serpent's suggestion that God is 'doing them down' by denying them the fruit. It is a temptation which goes to the heart of our incapacity for trust.

Jesus' temptations recapitulate our essential sinfulness: where we so often succumb, he has withstood. In our own desert he invites us to endure with him, to share in his reconciling work by saying 'Yes' with him to the Father's timing and ways.

But it is in the cross that we find the fullest meaning of our desert temptation and desolation. Jesus' refusal to pre-empt the Father's timing and to reinterpret his ways leads him to the hour when he experiences through and through what it is to be man without God. He who has waited upon his Father until this hour has again to wait upon a God who seems no longer there. Jesus is left to know the dread-full reality behind our desired independence from God which is at the heart of our sin. Pinned down as he is, without resources, without consolation, utterly unable to exercise our coveted autonomy, Jesus' desert is complete. As man without the Father he can do nothing, nothing but wait in that experience of being nothing, of being meaningless, which is the state of the godless. As St. Paul says:

For our sake God made him to be sin who knew no sin, so that in him we might become the righteousness of God.

(2 Corinthians 5:21)

Jesus takes all this into himself and returns it in himself to the Father so that everything in human experience is now in God, so that this experience of nothingness need no longer separate us from his love.

I have said earlier that our own experience of desert and darkness changes, that it moves from being our spiritual environment to being ourselves; we are the dry land, the stricken tree, the concrete desert of our imagining. Now we need to go a step further. In the cross Jesus has made our inner landscape his, too. He has become our wasteland, our blasted heath, so that he might also be our righteousness, our hope of glory. In the desert we are truly 'in Christ'.

For Jesus the desert and the dereliction of the cross were places where humankind, estranged from God, was reunited with the Father, where the 'golden ladder' between earth and heaven was restored.

He asks us not to 'go it alone' in our desert but to understand it as happening in him and with him, so that our movement back to the Father in this wasteland is part of the completion of his atoning work. He asks us to live, at a deeper level, what we have already glimpsed, the involvement of our personal imprisonment in darkness, rebellion, futility, with creation's groaning for liberation. He asks us to find the whole meaning for our lives in Paul's words to the Romans:

> *For the creation waits with eager longing for the revealing of the sons of God; for the creation was subjected to futility, not of its own will but by the will of him who subjected it in hope; because the creation itself will be set free from its bondage to decay and obtain the glorious liberty of the children of God.*
>
> *We know that the whole creation has been groaning in travail together until now; and not only the creation, but we ourselves, who have the first fruits of the Spirit, groan inwardly as we wait for adoption as sons, the redemption of our bodies. For in this hope we were saved. Now hope that is seen is not hope. For who hopes for what he sees? But if we hope for what we do not see, we wait for it with patience.*
>
> *(Romans 8:19–25)*

And so we can turn in our dry land to all those promises of redemption in the Old Testament with renewed confidence. We can be at peace, knowing that we, these deserts, will break out in flower, that we, who are all darkness, will become light, because we know that the dead wood of the cross has become

the tree of life, that the waste-place made of Jesus
has blossomed into eternal flower, that out of his
darkness pours an unquenchable light:

The wilderness and the dry land shall be glad,
the desert shall rejoice and blossom; ...
For waters shall break forth in the wilderness,
and streams in the desert;
the burning sand shall become a pool,
and the thirsty ground springs of water;
                                    (Isaiah 35:1, 6, 7)

Notes

CHAPTER 1 – Praying when God has gone away

1. The notion of a second conversion may puzzle some people. Conversion is a life-long process of being made into the person God has made us to be. There are high points in this process which are decisive for the nature of our journey to God; customarily these have been described as a second conversion.

2. 'Affliction 1' from *The Complete Poems of George Herbert*, edited by C.A. Patrides (London, J.M. Dent, 1974), p66.

3. 'No worst, there is none', from *The Poems of Gerard Manley Hopkins*, edited by W.H. Gardner (London, Penguin, 1967), p61.

CHAPTER 2 – For God alone my soul waits in silence

1. 'Come, let us sing a song unknown', from *Prayers of Charles de Foucauld* (New Jersey, Dimension Books), p3.

2. From *The Collected Works of St John of the Cross*, edited by Kieran Kavanaugh, Otilio Rodriguez (Washington, Institute of Carmelite Studies Publications, 1973), p103.

CHAPTER 3 – Strategies for Survival

1. Walter Hilton, *The Ladder of Perfection* (London, Penguin, 1957), p162.

2. The group traditionally known as the penitential Psalms are Psalms 6, 32, 38, 51, 102, 130 and 143.

Exploring Prayer

If you have found this book helpful, you may be interested in other titles in this collection edited by Joyce Huggett.

Angela Ashwin
PATTERNS NOT PADDLOCKS
Prayer for parents and all busy people, suggesting practical ideas and initiatives for prayer, building on the chaotic, busy-ness of everyday life.

James Borst
COMING TO GOD
A stage by stage introduction to a variety of ways of using times of stillness, quiet and contemplative meditation.

Michael Mitton
THE SOUNDS OF GOD
Helpful hints on hearing the voice of God, drawn from the contemplative, evangelical and charismatic traditions.

Heather Ward
STREAMS IN DRY LAND
Praying when God is distant, when you feel bored or frustrated with your prayer life – or even empty, arid and deserted by God.

COMING IN SEPTEMBER 1993

Joyce Huggett
FINDING GOD IN THE FAST LANE

Gerald O'Mahony
FINDING THE STILL POINT